LIVERPOOL
and the
Battle of the Atlantic 1939-45

Paul Kemp

...first ...s sunk within 12 hours of the declaration of war in 1939. The last ship was sunk 5 years, 8 months and 4 days later. During the Second World War over

4,700 allied and neutral merchant vessels were sunk and some

700 enemy submarines destroyed.

73,600 Royal Navy personnel,

30,000 merchant seamen and almost

6,000 from RAF Coastal Command perished, together with over

29,000 from enemy submarines.

£9.95

INTRODUCTION

The Battle of the Atlantic was undoubtedly the most important campaign of the Second World War. It is also the least understood. Britain needed food, munitions and raw materials with which to carry on the fight against Nazi Germany. There was no way that the need could be met from Britain's own resources so a tremendous amount of material had to be imported, mainly from Canada and the United States, by sea.

The Germans made considerable efforts to break this supply line. Using ships and aircraft, but mainly submarines, they attempted to sink the merchant ships, which, for their protection sailed in convoys under the watchful eye of warships. Had they succeeded in doing so, Britain would have been forced to surrender.

The Merseyside area lay at the heart of the battle. The Headquarters of Western Approaches Command were located in Liverpool and the warships used the nearby Gladstone dock as a base. Across the river at Birkenhead was the Cammell Laird shipyard which was busy building new warships as well as repairing those damaged in action. No finer description of Merseyside's role in the Battle of the Atlantic can be found than that written by Nicholas Montserrat in his epic novel **The Cruel Sea:**

Liverpool was a sailors; town and she went out of her way to make this generously plain. From the merchant ships lining the quays and docks, from the escorts cramming Gladstone dock, hundreds of men poured ashore every night, intent on enjoying their short hours of liberty: they got drunk, made disturbances, thronged the streets and the public houses, monopolised the prostitutes, seduced the young girls, and accommodated the married women – and Liverpool forgave them all and still offered her hospitality unstintingly. It was difficult to estimate the contribution to morale which Liverpool made, during this war-time invasion, but the happy background, the sure welcome, which continued for year after year, was a memorable help to sailors, giving them something to look forward to after weeks at sea.

The Battle of the Atlantic had few moments of great drama. Rather, it was a five year slog of attrition always played out against the foul weather of the North Atlantic. Yet it was a campaign that Britain had to win for her very survival. The photographs in this book show the convoys the escorts, the weapons, the conditions and some of the personalities involved. It also shows something of Merseyside's contribution to this great campaign.

What the Battle of the Atlantic was all about. A crated aircraft being unloaded at Liverpool. Note the "Made in USA" stencilled on the tail. Without American supplies of food, equipment and munitions Britain would have been unable to continue the war against Germany.

Shells being prepared for unloading. Every conceivable item of equipment came by sea from Canada and America.

4

An aerial view from an RAF Coastal Command aircraft of a 1943 convoy. Convoy, defined as "a group of merchant ships travelling together under escort", has provided the best means of defending maritime trade since the Middle Ages. If all the supplies carried by just one average sized Atlantic convoy (35 ships) were gathered together they would fill a line of ten ton trucks spaced 50 yards apart which would stretch from Inverness to Southampton via Carlisle.

July 1941. Before every convoy sailed the Masters of the merchant ships and the Commanding Officers of the escorting warships would meet for a pre-sailing conference. Details of signals and tactics would be discussed and grievances aired. These were the men who would "make it happen".

A merchant ship's Master takes notes at such a conference. Unlike their Royal Navy counterparts, Merchant Navy officers always wore civilian clothes to the pre-sailing conferences.

Another view of a convoy, taken early in the war – many of the ships are still wearing their peacetime liveries. The ships are in coastal waters, where attack was most likely to be expected in the early stage of war: Note the lifeboats swung out ready for immediate use.

A convoy on the high seas watched by Winston Churchill onboard HMS PRINCE OF WALES during his return from the Atlantic Meeting with President Roosevelt. Churchill, perhaps more than any other British politician realised the importance of maintaining the Atlantic sea route.

A view of a convoy taken from a destroyer in February 1942. Initially, escorts were only provided while the convoy was in the danger zone around the United Kingdom. Later in the war as the number of escorts available increased, convoys were escorted right across the Atlantic.

A Convoy Commodore on the bridge with the Master of the merchant ship. The convoy was the responsibility of the Commodore, usually a retired RN captain or junior flag officer, who sailed in one of the merchant ships. He directed the movements of the convoy as a whole but was not, however, in charge of the escorting warships. They were the responsibility of the senior officer of the escorts. ▶

The view of a convoy from a destroyer's (very) open bridge showing the Officer of the Watch and a lookout wearing foul weather clothing. Note the trawler in the background.

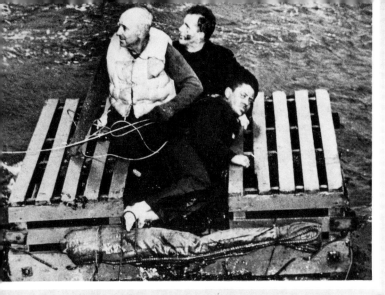

▲ Three British survivors from a torpedoed ship await rescue by a US Coastguard cutter. Their rescue was interrupted when a U Boat was detected in the area.

The cost of the battle: a tanker on fire after being shelled by a U-boat. This photograph was taken from a German cine film.

An Atlantic convoy at sunset seen from HMS VANOC in 1940. The Atlantic was not always so calm. VANOC was built in 1917 but pressed into service over 25 years later for Atlantic duty.

A different story… A merchant ship in foul weather. Not only did the convoys have to contend with the U-boat menace, there was the constant battle with the sea.

One of the Navy's "latest destroyers" in rough weather off Cape Wrath, Scotland in 1943 – heading into the North Atlantic.

HMS AMAZON rolling in heavy weather in 1941. Life onboard ship in such conditions could degenerate into the endless misery of continual watches, cold food, little sleep and constantly wet clothes – let alone the threat of U Boats.

A wave breaking over HMS AMAZON in 1941. In conditions like these, the after end of the ship was sometimes cut off since no man could retain his footing on the upper deck. Later in the war destroyers had flying bridges constructed to make fore and aft access a less perilous affair.

Winter in the North Atlantic: the Free French corvette LA RENONCULE ploughs through pancake ice during the winter of 1942/3.

Frozen spray on a destroyer's Hedgehog (Anti-submarine) launcher. Ice could build up on a ship's superstructure with potentially disastrous consequences.

December 1943. Working on the upper deck in such weather was dangerous. Here a Norwegian Navy depth charge party stand by the depth charge thrower in heavy weather.

HMS WALKER a member of the famous V&W class of destroyers was built in 1917 (by Denny). At the beginning of the war destroyers were the only type of ship available, in any numbers, for escort duty. Yet there were never enough of them. They were frequently needed for other purposes, and they were not suited to long distance escort work – they needed frequent refuelling.

HMS SHIKARI, built in 1919. Another old destroyer used as a North Atlantic convoy escort. This photograph shows her in the Mersey in 1944 by which time she had been much altered. Virtually all her gun armament was removed in favour of depth charges and other anti-submarine weapons. Note the depth charge racks, throwers and smoke floats at the stern. A radar lantern on a lattice mast replaced the pole mainmast and the foremast is fitted with radar. All this equipment gravely interfered with the ship's stability and there were fears for their safety in rough weather.

More escorts were needed... one of the ways of achieving this was to convert existing destroyers. Pre-war plans called for the conversion of the old ships of the V/W class to escort destroyers. The work was substantial and involved considerable structural alteration and complete re-arming with solely Anti-Aircraft (AA) and Anti-Submarine (ASW) weapons. This photograph shows HMS VANITY one of four ships to be converted.

The majority of the old destroyers were converted to Long Range Escorts (LRE). This is HMS VANESSA, another of the V/W class built in 1918. The conversion involved losing the forward boiler room and uptake to provide space for more fuel tanks. All the gun and torpedo armament was removed except for two 4" and one 3" gun and was replaced by depth charges and a Hedgehog ATW in place of "A" mounting. VANESSA'S increased endurance meant that she could stay with a convoy throughout its Atlantic voyage.

Despite their unsuitability, older fleet destroyers continued to work as convoy escorts throughout the war. This photograph shows HMS HESPERUS in the River Mersey with HMS LEEDS CASTLE (K.384) in the background.

A view of HOTSPUR, an H class destroyer which spent most of the war in Western Approaches Command. "A" and "Y" gun mountings have been replaced by a Hedgehog ATW (in the case of A) and more depth charges where "Y" gun would have been. One bank of torpedo tubes has been removed but the other retained – to fire the one ton depth charge.

Other types of vessel pressed into service as convoy escorts were trawlers such as this one, the KING SOL, seen on the Mersey in 1944. Trawlers proved very suitable as escorts because of their good seakeeping qualities and considerable endurance. Life onboard however, in a North Atlantic gale, must have driven men to the limits of their endurance.

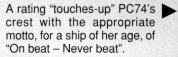

A rating "touches-up" PC74's crest with the appropriate motto, for a ship of her age, of "On beat – Never beat".

All ships that were of any use were pressed into service. HMS PC. 74 built in the First World War with a mercantile silhouette (to confuse U-boats) saw service as a convoy escort in the Second World War. Her armament consisted of little more than a large quantity of depth charges.

But it was to be through new construction that the shortage of the escorts was to be met. The first group of ships to be mass produced were the FLOWER class corvettes, subsequently immortalised in the novel **The Cruel Sea.** This photograph, taken in 1942, of HMS NASTURTIUM leading a convoy up the Mersey shows the corvette's simple design (based on a commercial whaler) and rudimentary armament.

HMS PENTSTEMMON bringing a convoy up the Mersey in 1943.

HMS HYDRANGEA, showing many wartime alterations and additions and the famous Liverpool skyline in 1944. Note the copious depth charge racks at the stern and the mast re-positioned aft of the bridge.

HMS BELLWORT approaching Victoria Wharf, Birkenhead on 11 May 1944.

HMS STORK, a BITTERNE class sloop. It is a popular misconception that destroyers were the most effective convoy escorts. Sloops provided better AA and ASW cover on a smaller hull which a destroyer could only match by being refitted out of recognition. This photograph shows STORK in July 1943 after considerable wartime modifications.

HMS ERNE, a BLACK SWAN class sloop, designed before the war as an ocean escort. These were seaworthy ships with an armament of six 4" guns and a considerable quantity of depth charges. Light AA guns varied in type and number throughout the war.

Some home coming... The sloop HMS WILD GOOSE enters Gladstone dock,
Liverpool on 25 February 1944 after an Atlantic Patrol.

35

HMS STARLING, forever famous as Captain F J Walker's ship in the 2nd Escort Group. STARLING was a modified BLACK SWAN class – built in response to growing demands for more escorts. The sloops were successful in their role but, since they were built to peacetime warship construction standards, were costly and took a long time to build. Something cheaper, more economical to construct but which carried the same "punch" was urgently required.

HMS ALNWICK CASTLE (November 1944) one of the CASTLE class of corvettes which were longer and more seaworthy than the FLOWERS. They carried an enhanced armament comprising a single 4" gun, a Squid Anti-Submarine mortar (mounted aft of, and above, the gun) and a large number of depth charges. The CASTLE class were introduced as a "stop gap" while new frigates were under construction. Their construction also kept yards which had built corvettes, but could not build the larger frigates, fully occupied.

HMS TEST originally called a twin screw corvette but later reclassified as a frigate. The River Class frigate represented the final design for an ocean going escort vessel. Armament consisted of two 4" guns, a Hedgehog launcher and 150+ depth charges.

The RIVER class frigate HMS SPEY in 1944 with a convoy.

Another RIVER class frigate, HMS ROTHER, heading downstream on the Mersey in 1945.

The Canadian RIVER class frigate HMCS LA HULLOISE approaches Gladstone dock in 1944.

HMS LOCH KILLIN photographed on completion. The RIVERS still took too long to build so the LOCH class were introduced. They carried a heavier armament, one 4" gun, two Squid launchers and depth charges. Their hulls were designed for rapid prefabrication.

K391

HMS LOCH TARBART leaving Gladstone dock in 1945.

HMS PADSTOW BAY, one of the BAY class which were AA variants of the LOCHS and designed to provide cover in areas where the air threat was considered more significant than that from U-Boats. The Squid launchers were not fitted but replaced by a second (twin) 4" mounting and extra light AA weapons.

The United States also supplied vital escorts under the lend-lease programme. Here are three CAPTAIN class frigates, HMS BERRY, DUCKWORTH AND ESSINGTON, which together with the similar COLONY class helped significantly to make up the numbers of escorts available for the North Atlantic.

Air support was vital to convoys. Aircraft extended the convoy's outer layer of defence by several hundred miles and proved invaluable in the reconnaissance role – as well as attacking and sinking U-boats. There were not enough fleet carriers to cover the Atlantic route so Escort Carriers were constructed from basic merchant ship hulls. The first, seen here, (HMS AUDACITY), was converted from the German merchant ship HANNOVER and proved her worth covering convoy HG76 in December 1941 before she was sunk.

HMS VINDEX an escort carrier completed in 1943 was converted from the merchant ship PORT VINDEX. Aircraft carried would be a mixture of Swordfish and Avengers. Most escort carriers were of US construction. Many problems were experienced with the early vessels.

Flying operations had to take place in all weathers. Here HMS BITER and HMS AVENGER pitch into a steep sea in the Atlantic in 1942. AVENGER was later lost.

Another photograph of escort carriers in heavy weather shows HMS EMPEROR and STRIKER , with an escorting destroyer, at sea during 1944.

Until sufficient escort carriers became available, a more ingenious conversion was the MAC Ship – (Merchant Aircraft Carrier) like the EMPIRE MACCOLL shown here. Bulk grain carriers or tankers were fitted with a flight deck and island which enabled them to carry aircraft in addition to their cargo carrying role.

EMPIRE MACRAE, another MAC ship with her convoy at the entrance to the Mersey in 1944. The MAC ship concept was a very successful marriage between the Royal and Merchant Navies – some aircrew had "Merchant Navy" painted on their aircraft instead of the more usual "Royal Navy".

Minesweepers (BRAMBLE and SPEEDY are seen here) played a vital but unsung role in the Battle of the Atlantic. As well as acting as escorts when occasions demanded, they performed the vital task of keeping the sealanes around Britain free of mines – as well as maintaining the British defensive minefields.

A Motor minesweeper (MMS) on the Mersey in 1942 with the Cathedral in the background. The censor has done his best to remove all items of minesweeping equipment but the acoustic hammer on the bow and the loop for sweeping magnetic mines on the stern can still be seen.

The depth charge was the chief weapon used against U-boats throughout the war. They could simply be dropped over the stern, as in this photograph from HMS SKATE, or thrown outwards by throwers. Two of the throwers can be seen at the bottom of the photograph – and on page 20.

The standard depth charge was the Mk.VIII which contained 290lbs of amatol. It could be set to explode at a pre-determined depth by means of a hydrostatic fuse and its descent to that depth was aided by a 150lb sinker. This photograph shows a depth charge being fitted to a thrower. Handling depth charges in heavy weather called for teamwork, co-ordination and training of a high order.

Depth charges, however, were unsatisfactory in that the ship had to run over the submerged submarine before she could drop them – and lost contact in the process. What was required was a weapon which threw the weapon ahead of the firing ship. The first of these was the Fairlie Mortar or the "Five Wide Virgins" shown fitted here to HMS WHITEHALL (July 1941). The weapon was not successful and did not enter operational service.

A salvo of twenty four Hedgehog bombs in flight. ▲

More successful was the Hedgehog which was a 24 spigot mortar, firing 65lb contact fused projectiles. They were arranged to give a 40 yard wide impact point – 200 yards ahead of the ship. They were not successful against deep targets. This photograph shows a trials mounting on HMS WESTCOTT.

HMS ESCAPADE after suffering an horrific accident in August 1943. Half the Hedgehog salvo exploded prematurely on being fired. The explosion demolished the mounting and wrecked the bridge – causing 22 casualties.

The "ultimate" Ahead Throwing Weapon (ATW) was the Squid, a three barrelled mortar in a frame which could be rotated through 90 degrees for loading. The projectiles carried a 207lb minol charge. Squid was fitted to all new construction frigates and corvettes. Its first successful use was by HMS LOCH KILLIN on 31 July 1944.

An aerial reconnaissance photograph of the Merseyside area showing the Liverpool/Bootle city centre, and the docks. This RAF mosaic photograph was taken on 26 October 1942.

Escorts, in this case HMS STARLING (left) and HMS WILD GOOSE (right), at the Gladstone Dock in Bootle. The Gladstone dock became "home" for the Western Approaches escort forces. These two vessels had just returned to Liverpool having sunk U202 in the Atlantic.

U45

"Wall to wall" warships. More escorts in the Gladstone Dock. From left to right: a CAPTAIN class frigate supplied under US lend-lease; a fleet destroyer and a sloop. Note the copious supplies of depth charges on the frigate's stern.

Gladstone dock was the scene of some memorable homecomings for the escorts. The damaged HMS HESPERUS enters the Dock on 28 December 1942 having rammed and sunk U.357 two days earlier during the passage of convoy HX.219. The "kill" was "shared" with HMS VANESSA. In the background is the Flower class corvette HMS MIGNONETTE.

A more detailed view of the damage to HESPERUS' bows. Ramming a U-boat was discouraged by the Admiralty as it meant that a valuable escort would be out of service whilst repaired for some time – taking up precious space in the shipyards. Under certain tactical conditions, however, ramming was the only option.

Two of HESPERUS' crew examine a Drager breathing apparatus –
part of the "loot" from U.357.

The Captain class frigate HMS AFFLECK (on 30 March 1944) after a memorable patrol with the 1st Support Group. During this patrol U.91 was sunk on 25 February and U.358 on 29 February 1944. However, the support group did not have things their own way for the destroyer GOULD had earlier been sunk by U.358.

HMS AYLMER, another CAPTAIN class frigate (at Holyhead) showing damage to her bows after ramming U.1051 on 26 January 1945. Subsequent repairs were undertaken at Gladstone Dock.

Two more detailed views of the damage to AYLMER's bows in dry dock. During the ramming it was reported by those on AYLMER's bridge that they could look down the U-boat's conning tower into her control room.

3 months later...
AYLMER's damage is
now fully repaired, the
anchor is being hoisted
– prior to the dock
being flooded up.

It's then back to the North Atlantic again. A fine view of AYLMER under way on the Mersey as she heads downstream for trials after repairs.

HMS DUCKWORTH after sinking U.480 on 24 February 1945. The kill was "shared" with HMS ROWLEY, another ship of the 3rd Escort Group. This photograph was taken at Belfast on 11 April 1944.

Members of DUCKWORTH's ship's company display their "Jolly Roger "showing the number of "kills" (together with the ship's emblem – naturally a Donald Duck!)

Inset: Captain Donald MacIntyre, an immensely successful escort commander who sank U.99, commanded by Kapitan-Leutnant Otto Kretschmer (one of the top scoring U-boat commanders) on 15 March 1941.

The Jolly Roger for the 3rd Escort Group of which DUCKWORTH was the senior ship, showing four kills. The crossed scalpels at the bottom left of the flag refer to two surgical operations successfully carried out at sea.

Of all the homecomings witnessed at Gladstone Dock the most memorable were those of Captain F J Walker's 2nd Escort Group. Walker, seen here (with sandwich) on the bridge of his ship, HMS STARLING, was one of the first naval officers to specialise in ASW and profited greatly from the systematic analysis of U-boat tactics emerging from the Western Atlantic Technical Unit (WATU).

Another typical photograph of Walker on the bridge during a U-boat hunt in 1944. Walker had already distinguished himself in HMS STORK sinking four U-boats in December 1941 during the passage of convoy HG.76. Appointed to HMS STARLING in 1943 he operated the 2nd Escort Group as an independent unit.

Undoubtedly Walker's greatest triumph was a patrol in February 1944 when his ships sank six U-boats. Three of the kills were made within a three hour period – proof of the efficacy of Walker's efforts. Here he stands on the bridge of HMS STARLING on 25 February 1944 acknowledging the welcome from a crowd of sailors and Wrens – and the First Lord of the Admiralty himself.

After the 2nd Escort Group Walker was due to command an escort carrier. He died however of a heart attack in 1944, undoubtedly brought on by strain and overwork, before he could take up the appointment. Here his coffin is brought onboard HMS HESPERUS for burial at sea.

The last Farewell... Top Naval, military and civilian dignitaries salute as HESPERUS pulls away from the Liverpool Pierhead.

The moment of committal: Walker's widow and daughter Gillian (in Wrens uniform) stand directly behind the coffin.

The amount of repair work handled by the various repair yards on Merseyside was enormous. Here the battleship HMS DUKE OF YORK and the Dutch destroyer ISAAC SWEERS share a dry dock at Cammell Laird's Birkenhead yard in 1944.

All kinds of work was undertaken. This photo-graph shows the damaged bows of the battle-ship HMS KING GEORGE V after she had rammed (and sunk) the destroyer HMS PUN-JABI in April 1942.

Some months later, the bows are completely repaired. Note the external de-gaussing cable. (KGV was the only ship of her class to have the cable on the outside of the hull).

The MAC (Merchant Aircraft Carrier) EMPIRE
MACALPINE in dock. MAC ships, which carried a small number of Swordfish aircraft
together with a bulk grain or oil cargo were a
most successful marriage of warship and
cargo vessel.

Boiler cleaning was the most frequent reason for a ship's maintenance period. Boilers needed cleaning at regular intervals, which also provided opportunities to send the ship's company on leave and to fit new weapons and equipment. Here, three stokers are inside the steam drum of a destroyer's boilers.

Boiler cleaning was necessary but unpleasant. A stoker, suitably clad, climbs into the water drum on one of a destroyer's boilers.

The same stoker, after the job was done, with his brush. Not a job for the claustrophobic!

Cleaning the funnel uptake on the destroyer, HMS PATHFINDER. Another filthy job, but one that was at least in the fresh air.

Fitting a complete new stern to an unidentified warship at the yard of Grayson Rolls, Sandhill on Merseyside in 1944.

HMS DUKE OF YORK leaving the Gladstone Dock in 1944 after a refit.

The people of Liverpool paid the price for its role as one of Britain's major ports – and home for the headquarters of Western Approaches Command. This photograph shows the junction of Lord Street, South Castle Street and Pressons Row after an air raid.

It was no better across the River Mersey. Damage in Livingstone Road, Birkenhead after a raid in 1940.

This view from the National Bank Buildings showing the burnt out Corn Exchange (with the Liver Birds in the background) after a raid on 3 May 1941. This period became known as "May Week" when the city was specially targeted by the Luftwaffe.

Damage to a residential area in Bootle after one of the "May Week" raids. Needless casualties were caused because the municipal authorities in Liverpool, Birkenhead and Bootle could not agree on a common civil defence plan.

January 1942 – Morale boosting: Admiral Sir Percy Noble (Commander in Chief) and the Lord Mayor of Liverpool inspect a Royal Marine band which gave a series of lunchtime concerts to shipyard and dock workers.

Admiral Sir Percy Noble, always known for his immaculate appearance, was the first Commander-in-Chief Western Approaches. He is seen here addressing the ships company of HMS STORK after their successful sinking of U.574.

The man most associated with Western Approaches Command was Admiral Sir Max Horton. A submariner of First World War vintage, he was appointed on the principle of "set a thief to trap a thief". He is shown at his office in his underground headquarters at Derby House, Liverpool.

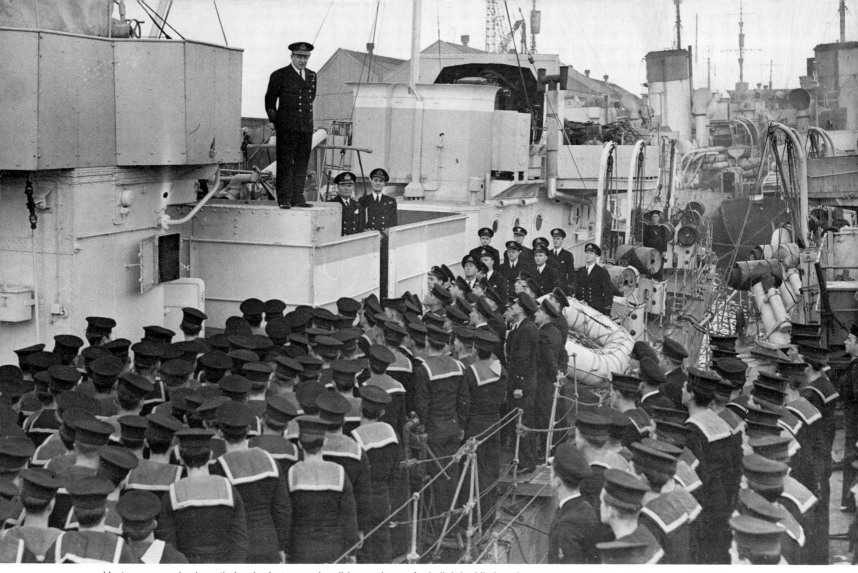

Horton was a charismatic leader but one who did not tolerate fools lightly. His headquarters was reported to be a model of inter-service co-operation. He is shown here addressing the ships' companies of HMS HESPERUS and HMS VANESSA after their sinking of U.356 in December 1942.

The operations room at Derby House, the HQ of Western Approaches Command, showing the gigantic plot which showed the movements of every convoy, escort group, straggler and U-boat.

An RNVR Lieutenant updates convoy movements on the plot at Derby House. In this case he is adjusting the position of a WN (Loch Ewe to Methil) convoy. Note the markers indicating the position of a homeward bound HX convoy from Halifax to the Clyde.

A WRNS rating updates the U-boat sighting plot at Derby House. Horton's headquarters was unique in the number of women filling important operation-related posts. This picture was taken for the benefit of the admiralty photographer – the U-boat reported "sunk" was fictional. ▶

Captain Gilbert Roberts, head of the Western Approaches Tactical Unit (WATU). The unit was set up by Admiral Noble to develop tactics to counter the U-boat menace. Roberts, like Walker, was an officer who had been retired between the wars through ill-health and, though he never went to sea, his contribution to the final victory was inestimable.

WRNS ratings lay out the track of a convoy, escorts and U-boats before a "battle" at the WATU training centre in Liverpool. Escort Group and individual ship commanders were given courses at WATU to sharpen their skills and inform them of the latest developments at sea.

An RN Reserve Lieutenant Commander peers through the screen at WATU to examine the tactical problem on the floor which he had to solve. The courses were tough and the WRNS, officers and ratings who ran them grew very competent at escort tactics. The lessons learned at these sessions were to be invaluable when applied at sea.

Merseyside spawned a number of shore establishments in the area. Here, Admiral Noble inspects a guard of honour at HMS VALKYRIE, the radar training school at Douglas on the Isle of Man.

As well as being a convoy port, Liverpool also saw numerous troop and evacuation convoys leave from the port. Here two children await collection in Liverpool to join a ship which would take them to America, part of the Government's evacuation scheme for children.

AMERICAN COMMITTEE FOR THE EVACUATION OF CHILDREN

BAGGAGE
TO BE
LEFT HERE

A troopship at the pierhead (20 June 1942) about to sail for the Middle East. For many of the troops lining the rails, this would be their last sight of England.

The liner MAURETANIA moves slowly downstream on 4 April 1945 carrying troops to the Far East.

Leaving the Gladstone dock, the destroyer HMS CARRON takes up station on the liner to act as her escort.

The hospital ship ATLANTIS approaches the pierhead (26 October 1943) with 790 repatriated British prisoners of war from Germany. These were men who had been captured in France, Greece or the Western Desert and who were judged, by the Red Cross, to be medically unfit to withstand the rigours of a PoW camp by virtue of their wounds.

A stretcher case comes ashore from the ATLANTIS. ▶

Liverpool's "friendly invasion" was American. Thousands of US troops came through Liverpool on their way to join formations building up for the Second Front. American soldiers form-up on the jetty at Liverpool after disembarking from the STIRLING CASTLE on 4 May 1944.

US troops on the landing stage waiting for a train to take them on to their destination. Note the guitar! This was well before the Beatles era too...

A welcome cup of coffee for two GIs given by
the American Red Cross.

Troops line the side of the MAURETANIA on her return to Liverpool from the Far East in September 1945. 5,800 troops were onboard – including 130 released prisoners of war, who were the first to come ashore.

Other arrivals at Liverpool, though in less happy circumstances, were hundreds of thousands of prisoners of war. Here some Italian soldiers, some of thousands captured in the early stages of the war in the western desert, come off a troopship at the Pierhead.

Clutching their meagre possessions they wait to board a train at the bombed out Riverside station.

Liverpool's most celebrated prisoner of war was undoubtedly Kapitan-leutnant Otto Kretschmer commanding officer of U.99 and one of the top-scoring U-boat commanders. Kretschmer's U.99 was sunk by HMS WALKER on 16 March 1941.

14 August 1942. U-boat prisoners were frequent arrivals at Liverpool. Here a gaggle of survivors from U.379 (sunk by HMS DIANTHUS on 8 August) passes an office advertising peacetime excursions to the Isle of Man on the Pierhead.

1943. A U-boat officer (blind-folded to prevent him observing naval installations in the port) is helped down the gangway.

U.532, a Type IX U-boat surrendered at Liverpool on 17 May 1945. She was the only U-boat to surrender at the port which had played such a part at ensuring victory.

A view of U.532 alongside the jetty with one of her cargo cylinders being removed. U.532 had returned from Japan with a cargo of strategic materials and arrived in home waters just in time to receive the order to surrender.

A dockyard matey inside on of U.532's cargo containers. Her cargo consisted of tin, quinine, wolfram and rubber – materials which were desperately needed by Germany's war effort.

Admiral Horton boarding U.532 for a visit on 18 May 1945 and being saluted by the submarine's commanding officer, Fregatten-Kapitan Ottoheinrich Junker. In the background are the escorts: HMS OXFORD CASTLE (K.692), HMS RUSHEN CASTLE (K.372), HMS FLINT CASTLE (K.383) and HMS KILMORE (U.15)